UNDERSTANDING EARTH'S SYSTEMS

Earth's Hydrosphere

AMY HAYES

PowerKiDS press

New York

Published in 2019 by The Rosen Publishing Group, Inc.
29 East 21st Street, New York, NY 10010

First Edition

Editor: Elizabeth Krajnik
Book Design: Rachel Rising

Photo Credits: Cover, p. 1 ZM_Photo/Shutterstock.com; pp. 3, 4, 6, 8, 10, 12, 14, 16, 18, 20, 22, 24, 26, 28, 30, 31, 32 Yellowj/Shutterstock.com; p. 5 titoOnz/Shutterstock.com; p. 7 PAUL ATKINSON/ Shutterstock.com; p. 9 Mykola Mazuryk/Shutterstock.com; pp. 10, 16, 27, 29 wizdata/Shutterstock.com; p. 11 NARISSARA BOONWISET/Shutterstock.com; p. 12 Reid Zandbelt/Shutterstock.com; p. 13 Courtesy of NASA Image and Video Library; p. 15 Yagi Studio/DigitalVision/Getty Images; p. 17 (top) Lars Christensen/Shutterstock.com; p. 17 (bottom) EddieCloud/Shutterstock.com; p. 19 Nattapol Sritongcom/Shutterstock.com; p. 20 fivepointsix/Shutterstock.com; p. 21 Darryl Brooks/ Shutterstock.com; p. 22 GoShiva/Shutterstock.com; p. 23 elenabsl/Shutterstock.com; p. 25 JEAN-FRANCOIS Manuel/Shutterstock.com; p. 27 Geography Photos/Universal Images Group/ Getty Images; p. 28 ChameleonsEye/Shutterstock.com; p. 29 polarman/Shutterstock.com; p. 30 studiovin/Shutterstock.com.

Cataloging-in-Publication Data

Names: Hayes, Amy.
Title: Earth's hydrosphere / Amy Hayes.
Description: New York : PowerKids Press, 2019. | Series: Understanding Earth's systems | Includes glossary.
Identifiers: LCCN ISBN 9781538329894 (pbk.) | ISBN 9781538329870 (library bound) | ISBN 9781538329900 (6 pack)
Subjects: LCSH: Water–Juvenile literature. | Hydrology–Juvenile literature. | Earth Science–Juvenile literature.
Classification: LCC GB662.3 H39 2019 | DDC 553.7–dc23

Manufactured in the United States of America

CPSIA Compliance Information: Batch #CS18PK: For Further Information contact Rosen Publishing, New York, New York at 1-800-237-9932

Contents

EARTH'S GLOBAL BALANCE 4

WATER, WATER EVERYWHERE 6

HOW THE HYDROSPHRE BEGAN . . . 8

THE OCEAN BLUE 10

LAKES 12

WATER BENEATH YOUR FEET 14

UP IN THE SKY 16

FORMING PRECIPITATION. 18

THE WORLD OF ICE. 20

THE WATER CYCLE 22

DANGEROUS WATERS 24

CHANGING THE MAKEUP
  OF WATER. 26

CLIMATE CHANGE 28

AN IMPORTANT RESOURCE. 30

GLOSSARY. 31

INDEX. 32

WEBSITES 32

Earth's Global Balance

Earth is a beautiful place with steep mountains, thick forests, and deep oceans. The planet is made of different systems, called **spheres**. The atmosphere is the whole mass of air that surrounds Earth. The biosphere is the part of the planet that contains living things. The geosphere is comprised of the solid layers of Earth. The hydrosphere includes all of the liquid, solid, and gaseous water on Earth. Each of these spheres has its own processes. However, they depend on each other and are very closely connected.

Every day, places on Earth experience different climates, seasons, and weather. This book focuses on the physical parts of the hydrosphere—oceans, lakes, rivers, groundwater, and **glaciers**—and also explores important processes in which water is involved.

All of Earth's systems work together to create balance. Even though each sphere is **unique**, they are interdependent. This means that changes in one sphere can cause changes in the others.

Water, Water Everywhere

The hydrosphere is all the water on Earth—solid, liquid, and gas. This includes water on Earth's surface, under the ground, and in the air. This is a lot of water! Water is the most **abundant** natural substance on our planet. It covers about 71 percent of Earth's surface.

The hydrosphere is made up of 326 million cubic miles (1.4 billion cubic kilometers) of water, which exists as oceans, lakes, streams, glaciers, and groundwater. Earth's oceans make up the greatest part of the hydrosphere (97.25 percent) while the water in rivers makes up one of the smallest parts of the hydrosphere (0.0001 percent).

Earth has two types of water: fresh water and salt water. Most of Earth's water—more than 96 percent—is salt water. Less than 4 percent of Earth's water is fresh water. Humans, land animals, and freshwater animals need fresh water to live.

Humans and animals can't drink salt water. However, **marine** life, like this angelfish, requires salt water for survival. If you put an angelfish in fresh water, it would die.

SYSTEM CONNECTIONS

Most of Earth's fresh water exists underground, not on Earth's surface in lakes and rivers.

How the Hydrosphere Began

Why does Earth have so much water? Where did it come from? Some scientists believe that as Earth was forming, there were many chemical reactions that created water. This water pushed up from the lower layers of Earth's interior to the surface, where it cooled on the surface instead of escaping out of the atmosphere. However, this idea is not as popular as it once was. Scientists don't think this explains the amount of water on Earth today.

Most scientists believe that long ago, asteroids and comets that contained ice repeatedly hit Earth. These scientists believe that a lot of the water on Earth's surface actually came from objects from other parts of the solar system.

SYSTEM CONNECTIONS

Theories are ideas intended to explain facts or events. Scientists never consider any ideas final because there's always a chance they can learn more about a subject.

The amount of water on Earth hasn't changed much since Earth's early history. Earth gains a small amount of water—about 0.07 cubic miles (0.3 cubic km) per year—through degassing. Degassing is when Earth's interior releases gas, creating water.

The Ocean Blue

Oceans are a huge part of Earth's hydrosphere. Scientists estimate that oceans contain more than 96 percent of Earth's water, which is about 324 million cubic miles (1.35 billion cubic km) of water. According to modern-day boundaries, there are five oceans on Earth: the Atlantic, Pacific, Arctic, Indian, and Southern. However, if you look at a map or a globe, you can see that these oceans are all connected, making them one huge body of water. This is sometimes called the Global Ocean.

Water is made up of two hydrogen **molecules** and one oxygen molecule. However, ocean water also has some substances that make it different from water found in other parts of the hydrosphere. Sodium, chlorine, magnesium, and sulfate are the four most common substances found in sea water.

Keeping Us Warm

Oceans play an important role in keeping Earth warm enough for life to survive. Oceans absorb, or take in, much more heat from the sun than the land or the atmosphere do. As the sun warms the oceans, they keep a lot of that heat instead of bouncing the heat back into space. This warms Earth. As the currents of the ocean move around Earth, this heat is sent to different parts of the world.

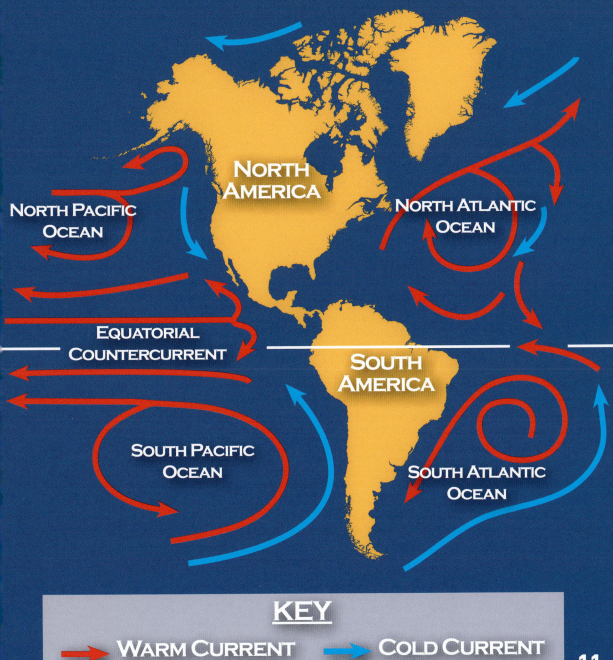

Currents move ocean water around Earth. These currents affect the weather in many places.

NORTH
AMERICA

NORTH PACIFIC
OCEAN

NORTH ATLANTIC
OCEAN

EQUATORIAL
COUNTERCURRENT

SOUTH
AMERICA

SOUTH PACIFIC
OCEAN

SOUTH ATLANTIC
OCEAN

KEY

→ WARM CURRENT   → COLD CURRENT

Lakes

Lakes are bodies of water that exist on every continent. They come in all sizes, depths, and elevations. Using photos taken from space, a team of scientists found that there are about 117 million lakes on Earth. Most lakes contain fresh water. However, there are some saltwater lakes. All freshwater lakes are open, which means that a body of water flows into or out of them. A lake is closed if water only leaves it by evaporation. Closed lakes often become saltwater lakes.

Runoff, groundwater seepage, glaciers, earthquakes, and volcanic activity can all form lakes. Sometimes rivers create lakes. Because lakes depend on runoff, they can change a lot in size and temperature due to the weather or the season.

Lake Baikal in Siberia, Russia, is the oldest and deepest freshwater lake on Earth. At its deepest point, Lake Baikal is 5,315 feet (1,620 m) deep and holds one-fifth of Earth's fresh water—5,500 cubic miles (23,000 cubic km).

Water Beneath Your Feet

In many places, water can't be seen, but water flows beneath our feet. Groundwater is an important part of Earth's hydrosphere. About 30 percent of liquid fresh water comes from groundwater. Groundwater seeps through spaces between rocks under the soil. A layer of rock or sand that can absorb, or take in, and hold water is called an aquifer.

Aquifers are a key source of drinking water. Many people dig or drill deep holes in the ground to reach the water stored in an aquifer. These deep holes are called wells. A well pulls up fresh water from an aquifer for people to use. Water that isn't pulled up continues to slowly seep through rocks, creating pathways under our feet to larger water sources such as rivers and lakes.

SYSTEM CONNECTIONS

Aquifers are a good source of fresh water, but pumping up too much too quickly can make a well run dry.

This old-fashioned pump brings water to the surface from the well below.

Up in the Sky

Do you ever spend time watching the clouds go by in the sky? Just like the rain and the snow that come from them, clouds are made of water. This means clouds are part of the hydrosphere as well as the atmosphere.

When water is warmed to a certain temperature, it evaporates. Evaporation is the process by which water changes from a liquid to a gas. Even though water moves from Earth's surface to the atmosphere as vapor, it remains a part of the hydrosphere. Like the oceans, water vapor traps heat and keeps the air warm. When this vapor travels high into the sky, it sticks to tiny pieces of dust and ice and **condenses** into tiny droplets too small to see.

What Is Fog?

When a cloud is low enough to the ground, it's called fog. There are several different types of fog. Radiation fog, or ground fog, forms in the evening or at night when the heat from the ground is radiated, or sent out, into the air. This type of fog can stay until morning, when it is said to be "burned off" by the heat from the sun—meaning the condensed water evaporates back into vapor.

Big, fluffy clouds are called cumulus clouds.

17

Forming Precipitation

Precipitation is water that falls from clouds to Earth's surface as rain, freezing rain, snow, sleet, or hail. However, most precipitation occurs as rain. When small droplets of water evaporate into the atmosphere and condense, they stick to small particles of dust and other things in the air. These small droplets aren't yet heavy enough to fall as precipitation. Over time, they get bigger and heavier and fall to the ground.

Temperature is another important reason precipitation occurs. Warm air can hold a lot more water vapor than cold air can. When warm air mixes with cold air, the temperature of the vapor lowers and it condenses, forming more big droplets. That's why it rains when cold air and warm air meet.

SYSTEM CONNECTIONS

The highest average annual rainfall is 467 inches (11,873 mm), in Meghalaya, India.

The biosphere, or the part of Earth in which life can exist, depends on precipitation as a source of water. For life to exist, there must be liquid water.

The World of Ice

The ice and snow on Earth's surface make up the cryosphere, which is part of the hydrosphere. *Cryosphere* comes from the Greek word *krios*, which means "cold." The cryosphere exists on Earth as glaciers, ice caps, ice sheets, snow, and permafrost. The ice found in water, including the frozen parts of oceans, lakes, and rivers, is also part of the cryosphere.

Ice makes up just over 2 percent of Earth's hydrosphere. That may sound like a very small amount, but it's almost 7 million cubic miles (29 million cubic km). Ice that stays frozen all throughout the year plays an important part in regulating Earth's atmosphere. Because ice is so reflective, much of the energy from the sun that hits ice is bounced back into space. This helps keep Earth cool.

Hubbard Glacier, a tidewater glacier off the coast of Yakutat, Alaska, is more than 6 miles (9.7 km) wide where it meets the ocean. Its face reaches up to 400 feet (122 m) tall.

Drilling into the Past

When ice forms, solids and gases get trapped in the ice. As layer after layer forms over thousands of years, these pieces of matter stay where they are. Scientists who want to learn more about Earth's past drill down and take out long tube-shaped samples of ice called ice cores. They then study the matter in the ice cores to find out what Earth's climates used to be like thousands—and even millions—of years ago.

The Water Cycle

Oceans, lakes, clouds, rain, groundwater, runoff, and glaciers all play an important role in the water cycle. During the water cycle, water is circulated between Earth's oceans, atmosphere, and land. This cycle is one of the key processes that takes place in Earth's hydrosphere.

There are several steps in the water cycle. Water in the ocean or on land is warmed by the sun's rays. It evaporates into vapor. Wind carries the vapor as a cloud. The vapor condenses and falls to Earth's surface as precipitation. The water may soak into the soil, or it may be added to the other surface water that makes up lakes, rivers, or streams. From a river, stream, or runoff, the water moves to a lake or back to the ocean.

THE WATER CYCLE

Dangerous Waters

While water is necessary for life on Earth to exist, water—in all its forms—can also be dangerous. Blizzards, flash floods, thunderstorms, and tsunamis are just some of the ways in which the hydrosphere can cause problems. Some of the most dangerous hydrospheric events are hurricanes and tsunamis. Hydrospheric events can also cause problems in Earth's other spheres, such as heavy rains causing landslides in the geosphere.

A tropical cyclone, called a hurricane in the north Pacific and Atlantic Oceans, is an atmospheric weather event that forms over warm tropical oceans. These violently rotating storms spin around a center of low atmospheric presure, known as the eye. High winds push the storm toward land, often causing storm surges, which are higher levels of sea water that can cause severe flooding.

Hurricanes can cause a great deal of damage. This image shows the aftermath of Hurricane Maria on the island of Dominica on September 18, 2017. Dominica is part of a chain of islands located in the southeastern part of the Caribbean Sea.

SYSTEM CONNECTIONS

For a storm to be called a hurricane, winds must reach 74 miles (119 km) per hour.

Changing the Makeup of Water

Human activities affect the hydrosphere. When people pollute water, the hydrosphere is negatively affected. Toxic waste from factories and other harmful substances can leak into water supplies and cause plants, animals, and humans to get sick and even die.

Fertilizer is used on farms that grow food and on people's lawns. When it runs off into surface water, fertilizer can cause many problems. One problem is called **eutrophication**. This happens when water has a lot of nitrogen and phosphorous. The excess nitrogen and phosphorous cause plants to grow abnormally fast. This is a bad thing because the plants use up all the oxygen in the water, which leaves very little for the other life-forms living in the water.

This drainage ditch is experiencing eutrophication, which has caused algae to grow too fast. The algae choke the rest of the life in the water because it blocks out sunlight and uses up much of the oxygen in the water to create its food.

Acid Rain

When **fossil fuels** are burned, harmful chemicals are released into the atmosphere. These chemicals can mix with water vapor and change the makeup of water, turning it acidic. When the acid rain falls to Earth, it causes problems. Acid rain can fall anywhere, but it happens most often in places that have a lot of factories. Forests, lakes, streams, and people with asthma or other breathing issues can be hurt by acid rain. It can even cause paint to peel.

Climate Change

Most scientists agree that climate change is caused by human activities. Factories, cars, and large farms release **greenhouse gases** into the atmosphere. These gases stay in the atmosphere and act like the roof of a greenhouse, trapping heat from sunlight in the atmosphere. This causes Earth's surface and atmosphere to have a higher average temperature.

The hydrosphere has been negatively affected by the increase in average global temperature. Much of our planet's sea ice used to stay frozen all year. But this important part of the cryosphere has been melting more and more. This can raise the sea level around the world. The higher the sea level, the more floods there will be.

These scientists are measuring and taking samples of the water in Antarctica. Collecting data is important for studying changes in the hydrosphere.

Global Warming and Cold Days

Global warming is the rapid increase in average temperature around the world in recent years. However, this doesn't mean that every part of the world has warmer weather every day. Weather describes daily conditions like rain and temperature in localized areas. Climate is the average weather of a place over a period of years. So, while it may be a cold day outside, that doesn't mean the average temperature of your area hasn't increased.

29

An Important Resource

The hydrosphere is everywhere—from the water you drink to the water in the air and under your feet. As Earth's most plentiful resource, water plays an important role in keeping Earth balanced. The cryosphere helps keep Earth from getting too hot, while the oceans help keep Earth from getting too cold.

Rain, aquifers, and lakes are all necessary resources in supporting life on Earth. Even though water can be dangerous, it is important to realize that even on a day without a cloud in the sky, the hydrosphere works to keep Earth's weather and climate regulated.

The next time you get a drink of fresh water, think about the journey that water has taken and the ways people can protect this valuable resource.

abundant: Existing in large amounts.

condense: To change from a gas to a liquid.

eutrophication: The enrichment of an aquatic ecosystem, such as a lake, with chemical nutrients, which causes an overgrowth of plant life and a decreased oxygen level in the water.

fossil fuel: A fuel—such as coal, oil, or natural gas—that is formed in the earth from dead plants or animals.

glacier: A large body of ice moving slowly down a slope or valley or spreading outward on a land surface.

greenhouse gases: The gases that absorb energy from sunlight, trap heat in the atmosphere, and are part of the greenhouse effect.

marine: Relating to the sea or the plants and animals that live in the sea.

molecule: The smallest possible amount of something that has all the characteristics of that thing.

runoff: Water from rain or snow that flows over the surface of the ground into bodies of water, such as lakes, streams, or oceans.

sphere: An area of activity, existence, or authority. It also means an object shaped like a ball.

unique: Being the only one of its kind.

Index

A
acid rain, 27
aquifers, 14, 30
atmosphere, 4, 8,
     16, 20, 28

B
biosphere, 4

C
climate change,
     21, 28, 29
clouds, 16, 18, 22
condensation, 16,
     18, 22
cryosphere, 20, 28, 30

E
eutrophication, 26
evaporation, 12, 16,
     18, 22

F
fog, 16
fresh water, 6, 7,
     12, 14, 30

G
geosphere, 4, 24
glaciers, 4, 6, 12,
     20, 22
Global Ocean, 10
global warming, 29
greenhouse gases,
     28
groundwater, 4, 6,
     12, 14, 22

H
hurricanes, 24, 25
hydrosphere
     beginning of, 8
     and climate
        change, 28–29
     dangerous events,
        24
     definition, 6
     percent of fresh
        and salt water, 6
     pollution of, 26
     total water in, 6

I
ice, 8, 16, 20, 21, 28
ice cores, 21

L
lakes, 12, 20, 22, 30
landslides, 24

O
oceans, 4, 6, 10, 20,
     22, 24, 30

P
precipitation, 18, 22

R
runoff, 12, 22

S
salt water, 6, 12
spheres, 4

T
tropical cyclone, 24
tsunamis, 24

W
water cycle, 22

Websites

Due to the changing nature of Internet links, PowerKids Press has developed
an online list of websites related to the subject of this book. This site is updated
regularly. Please use this link to access the list: www.powerkidslinks.com/ues/hydro